Henrietta L. Sawtelle

What one can do with a chafing Dish

a guide for amateur Cooks

Henrietta L. Sawtelle

What one can do with a chafing Dish
a guide for amateur Cooks

ISBN/EAN: 9783744789929

Printed in Europe, USA, Canada, Australia, Japan

Cover: Foto ©Andreas Hilbeck / pixelio.de

More available books at **www.hansebooks.com**

WHAT ONE CAN DO WITH A CHAFING-DISH

A Guide for Amateur Cooks

By H. L. S.

NEW REVISED AND ENLARGED EDITION
TWENTIETH THOUSAND

Contents.

	PAGE		PAGE
Anchovy Toast, Creamed,	148	Calf's Liver Sauté,	82
Articles convenient to have for Chafing-dish,	5	Caviare,	149
		Cheese Croûton,	141
		Cheese Fondu,	140
Beans, Lima,	114	Cheese Soufflé,	142
Beef, Cold Roast, Réchauffé of,	66	Chicken à la Reine,	95
Beef, Chipped,	63	Chicken, Canned,	98
Beef, Curry of Cold Roast,	65	Chicken, Salpicon of,	97
Beef en Matelotte,	62	Chicken Terrapin,	96
Beef with Jelly,	69	Chops with Mushrooms,	72
Beefsteak à la Mode,	59	Clams,	20
Beefsteak Réchauffé,	60	Clams and Scallops, Creamed,	22
Beignets de Pommes,	145	Clams, Soft-shell,	21
Bouchés D'Huîtres,	44	Collops, Minced au Naturel,	64
Bouille-à-Baisse,	31	Crabs en Crême,	53
Bread Sauté,	146	Crabs, Sauté,	52
Bubble and Squeak,	67	Curry Sauce for Cold Meats,	90

1

CONTENTS.

	PAGE		PAGE
Dried Beef with Eggs,	127	Fish, Salt Cod, Dessicated,	33
Duck, Canvas-back,	94	Fish, Salt Cod, Hash,	36
		Fish, Salt, Scorched,	32
Eggs à l'Espagnole,	133	Fish, White, à la Provençale,	41
Eggs à la Jardinière,	128	Fricandeau de foie de veau,	83
Eggs à la Maître D'Hôtel,	135	Fritadella,	91
Eggs, Creamed,	134	Frogs,	58
Eggs, Curried,	131		
Eggs, Fricasseed,	132	Game, Salmi of,	102
Eggs, Scrambled,	136	Game, Salpicon of,	105
Eggs en huile, Scrambled,	137		
		Ham à l'Espagnole,	88
		Ham à la Fourchette,	87
Fish, Cod, Deviled,	38	Ham and Eggs,	138
Fish, Cod, Scrambled,	35	Ham, Deviled,	86
Fish, Cod, Tongues,	37	Ham, Piquant Sauce,	89
Fish, Curried,	30	Hamburg Steak,	61
Fish—Halibut Sauté,	40	Huîtres en Coquilles,	49
Fish—Herring à l'Anglaise,	55		
Fish, Réchauffé of,	28	Jambon à bon goût,	109
Fish Roe,	27		
Fish Roe, Shad, Curried,	54	Lamb's Liver,	84
Fish, Salpicon of,	34	Lobster,	25

CONTENTS.

	PAGE		PAGE
Lobster à la Newberg,		Oysters, Kornlet,	48
Lobster au Naturel,	24	Oysters, Sautés,	45
Lobster, Curried,	23	Oysters, Scolloped,	46
	26		
Macaroni à la Gruyère,	144	Petit Pois,	110
Macaroni au Gratin,	125	Pic-ca-dee,	101
Mushrooms—Agaricus Campestris	120	Pig's Feet Sauté,	85
Mushrooms à la Provençale,	124	Potatoes à la Lyonnaise,	112
Mushrooms — Cantharellus Cibarius,	122	Potatoes Réchauffé,	113
		Potato Soufflé,	111
Mushrooms — Fairy Ring Champignon,	121	Poulet au Champignons,	100
		Preface,	7
Mushrooms, Meadow,	118	Prune Toast,	147
Mushroom Puff Ball,	119		
Mushrooms, Sauté of,	117	Ragoût of Cold Meat,	70
Mushrooms with Bacon,	123	Reed Birds,	107
Mutton or Lamb Réchauffé,	71	Reed Birds in Blankets,	108
Mock Oyster Stew,	50		
		Salmon à la Reine,	29
Omelet,	129	Salmon Réchauffé,	39
Omelet, Tomato,	130	Salpicon Imperial	99
Oyster Crabs, Sauté of,	51	Sardine Toast,	56
Oysters à la Crême,	47		

CONTENTS.

	PAGE		PAGE
Sardines with Hollandaise Sauce,	57	Tomatoes, Fried,	115
Scallops and Clams, Creamed,	22	Tongue, Deviled Ox.	79
Scallops en huile,	43	Tripe,	92
Scallops, Sauté of,	42	Tripe Sauté,	93
Shrimps,	17	Turkey, Capilotade of	104
Shrimps, Creamed,	18	Turkey, Salpicon of,	103
Shrimps, Stewed,	19		
Squabs,	106	Veal, Curried,	77
Stew, English,	68	Veal Cutlets,	76
Sweet-breads,	75	Veal Kidneys Sauté,	78
Sweet-breads à la Milanaise,	73	Venison,	80
Sweet-breads and Mushroom Ragoût,	74	Venison Steak,	81
		Welsh Rarebit,	139
Tomato Purée and Macaroni,	126	Welsh Rarebit, Paprica.	143
Tomatoes and Mushrooms,	116	Wheatena,	150

List of Articles Convenient to Have on Hand for Chafing-Dish Use.

Tomato Purée. (Italian grocer.)
Johnston's Fluid Beef. (Any good grocer.)
Anchovy paste.
Paprica (Hungarian red pepper).
Curry powder.
Kornlet.
Caviare.
Garlic.
Can of unsweetened condensed milk.
Mushroom catsup.
Tomato catsup.
Petit Pois.
Two or three small wooden spoons.
A small grater.
Wire-toaster for gas.

PREFACE.

CHAFING-DISHES are growing daily more and more in favor, and to the daintiness of the food to be prepared is added the charm of social intercourse and the informality of the environment. The excellence of the edibles so prepared lies greatly in the fact that they are served instantly, and that the hand of the cook is guided by brains. Many dainty dishes lose much of the piquancy of their flavor in the transfer from the kitchen range to the dining-room.

Lalance & Grosjean have added to their outfit of agate utensils a small stove, heated by a remarkable fuel called Sestalit, which emits no smoke or odor, is cleanly and non-explosive, and creates no flame.

It will be found a most convenient addition to the usual alcohol lamp, and in many instances will take the place of it. The heat is moderate and uniform. It is often desirable to keep one dish hot while another is being prepared, and in cooking mushrooms a low temperature is essential, in order to preserve their delicate flavor. This mode of cooking is also very inexpensive, as two cents' worth of the fuel will keep the chafing-dish supplied for at least two hours.

I also recommend a small wire arrangement for toasting bread by the heat of a gas-burner. The use of this recent invention (which can probably be found at any of the house-furnishing stores) enables one to have hot toast to be served with the contents of the chafing-dish.

IT will be noticed that the recipe used almost invariably for the chafing-dish source, is two tablespoonfuls of flour, mixed smoothly with two tablespoonfuls of melted butter; the spoonfuls of flour should be scant, even tablespoonfuls, and those of butter, heaping. Good stock can be made at a moment's notice by dissolving a dessert-spoonful of fluid beef in half a pint of boiling water, well seasoned with pepper, salt, and two or three drops of extract of celery, and a small teaspoonful of onion juice.

I ESPECIALLY recommend the use of Johnston's Fluid Beef for stock and sauces. It is an extract of the choicest beef, prepared (under letters patent) with scrupulous care, and is not only nutritive, but very palatable. It has a much more agreeable flavor than any of the other condensed preparations of beef, and for chafing-dish use it will be found to be almost indispensable, as many of the recipes depend for their excellence partly upon this invaluable preparation.

"THE spirit of each dish, and zest of all,
  Is what ingenious cooks the relish call,
For though the market sends in loads of food,
They are all tasteless, till that, makes them good."

—Kings Cookery.

THIS foretaste of Epicurean delights I dedicate to an old friend in the Admiralty, the delicacy of whose gastronomic perceptions is the best authority I can offer, for the excellency of these recipes.

"HE that can grasp the golden mean,
And is content to live between
　　The little and the great—
Knows not the wants that plague the poor,
Nor the plagues that fret the rich man's door."
　　　　　　　　　—Horace.

———

"HE that will have a cake out of wheat, must needs tarry at the grinding."—Troilus and Cressida.

"WE may live without poetry, music and art,
 We may live without conscience, and live without heart;
We may live without friends, we may live without books,
But civilized man cannot live without cooks!

He may live without books—what is knowledge but grieving?
He may live without hope—what is hope but deceiving?
He may live without love—what is passion but pining?
But where is the man that can live without dining?"

"WHAT does cookery mean? It means the knowledge of Medea, and of Circe, and of Calypso, and of Helen, and of Rebekah, and of the Queen of Sheba. It means knowledge of all herbs, and fruits, and balms, and spices, and of all that is healing and sweet in groves, and savory in meat. It means carefulness and inventiveness, watchfulness, willingness, and readiness of appliances. It means the economy of your great-grandmother, and the science of modern chemistry, and French art, and Arabian hospitality. It means, in fine, that you are to see imperatively that every one has something nice to eat."—RUSKIN.

It means, also, that much may be done by taking pains with a chafing-dish.

AN Agate Chafing-Dish, of extra size, is manufactured expressly for the recipes contained in this book, and it is preferable to any other (except sterling silver), not only on account of the smooth, polished surface, but the much greater amount of heat to be obtained quickly.

SHRIMPS.

PUT into the chafing-dish two tablespoonfuls of butter, half an onion, grated or minced very fine. When hot, stir in half a cup of cold rice, carefully boiled; add a gill of cream, and half a pint of canned or fresh shrimps; add a tablespoonful of tomato sauce. Stir well until it comes to the boiling point, then let it simmer for about five minutes.

Creamed Shrimps.

ONE can of shrimps, half a pint of cream, a teaspoonful of paprica, a little salt, and a little nutmeg. Cut the shrimps in small pieces; put all together in the chafing-dish, stir constantly, and when it comes to a boil (do not let it boil actively) stir in two well-beaten eggs and a glass of Moselle.

Stewed Shrimps.

Put in the chafing-dish two tablespoonfuls of butter; when melted, stir in a tablespoonful of flour, a little salt and pepper. Add gradually nearly a pint of rich milk. Rinse in cold water a can of N. O. shrimps, dry them, cut in two, and add them to the sauce. Stir constantly for four or five minutes, and serve hot.

CLAMS.

HAVE twenty-five clams chopped fine; put in the chafing-dish two tablespoonfuls of butter; when melted, add two tablespoonfuls of flour. Add the clams, with half a pint of their juice; season well with pepper and salt, and let them simmer from ten to fifteen minutes. Just before serving, add a gill of cream, and let it come to a boil; serve hot.

Soft-shell Clams.

Have all the hard part removed from fifty perfectly fresh soft-shell clams. Put in the chafing-dish a heaping tablespoonful of butter; when melted, add the clams, with a wineglass of Madeira. Let them cook *slowly* for about ten minutes. Add the well-beaten yolks of three eggs to a pint of cream, pour this over the clams, and stir constantly for about five minutes.

Scallops and Clams Creamed.

ONE bunch of soft-shell clams from which the hard part has been carefully removed; one-half pint of scallops. Let the scallops stand in very hot water for five minutes, then drain. Put in the chafing-dish two tablespoonfuls of butter; when melted, add a tablespoonful of flour, a little pepper and salt, and a few drops of onion-juice; stir in a gill of cream. When very hot, add the clams and scallops, and cook from five to ten minutes.

Lobster au Naturel.

BEAT the yolks of two eggs, with two tablespoonfuls of butter, until smooth; add a gill of cream; season well with pepper and salt; stir in the finely-chopped meat of a freshly-boiled lobster; let it simmer for a few minutes, and serve hot. Do not let it boil, as that would cook the egg too much.

LOBSTER À LA NEWBERG.

TAKE the nicest part of two small or one large lobster, cut into small slice, put in the chafing-dish with a tablespoonful of butter; season well with pepper and salt, pour over it a gill of wine; cook ten minutes; add the beaten yolks of three eggs and half a pint of cream. Let all come to a boil, and serve immediately.

LOBSTER.

CHOP or shred the meat of a cold, boiled lobster, tail and claws; pour over it the juice of two lemons, add half a teaspoonful of cayenne, and a teaspoonful of salt. Put in the chafing-dish three tablespoonfuls of fresh butter; when melted, add the lobster. Let it simmer for about ten minutes, stirring constantly.—CATERER.

CURRIED LOBSTER.

PUT in the chafing-dish a tablespoonful of butter, and fry an onion and an apple, chopped very fine, until they are thoroughly cooked; sprinkle with curry-powder, according to taste, from a teaspoonful to a tablespoonful; mix a tablespoonful of cornstarch with half a pint of cream; pour into the chafing-dish, and when it is smooth and very hot add the lobster, cut in small pieces.

Fish Roe.

Put two tablespoonfuls of butter in the chafing-dish, with a tablespoonful of vinegar or lemon juice. Add a shad roe (which has been previously boiled about ten minutes in salted water). Break up lightly with a fork, add the yolks of two hard-boiled eggs, mashed fine, a small cup of grated bread crumbs, a little chopped parsley, pepper and salt. Stir constantly until all is well mixed, and serve very hot.

Rechauffé of Fish.

Cut fine, any cold-boiled fish; put in the chafing-dish with two tablespoonfuls of butter; when melted, add a cupful of bread crumbs, two eggs beaten slightly, two tablespoonfuls of cream or milk, a teaspoonful of anchovy paste, a little pepper and cayenne. Mix all well together; let it simmer about five minutes, stirring constantly, and serve.

Salmon à la Reine.

Put two tablespoonfuls of butter in the chafing-dish; when melted, stir in gradually a tablespoonful of flour; stir until quite smooth; add a gill of water, the juice of a lemon, pepper, salt, a small onion, minced very fine or grated, and the yolks of three hard-boiled eggs, mashed fine. Add a can of salmon or a pound of fresh-boiled salmon; let it simmer about five minutes and serve.

Curried Fish.

COOK one tablespoonful of onion, cut very fine, in one tablespoonful of butter, five minutes. Be careful not to burn. Mix one tablespoonful of curry powder with one tablespoonful of flour, and stir into the melted butter. Add, gradually, half a pint of milk or cream, stirring constantly. Then add a large cupful of any kind of cold-boiled fish; let it simmer a few minutes. and serve very hot.

Bouille à Baisse.

Fry an onion chopped very fine in two tablespoonfuls of pure olive oil; add a clove of garlic minced very fine, a dash of cayenne, a teaspoonful of salt, a tablespoonful of flour; stir until smooth; then add half a pint of white stock, a cupful of cold boiled cod or halibut, a cupful of lobster; let it simmer from ten to fifteen minutes, stirring often.

Scorched Salt Fish.

PICK a small piece of the thickest part of a salt cod, which has been soaked over night, into long flakes; dry with a napkin; put in the chafing-dish two tablespoonfuls of butter; when *very hot*, put in the flakes of fish, brown a little on both sides; serve very hot. It is a good appetizer.

Salt Cod Fish, Desiccated.

Put in the chafing-dish two tablespoonfuls of butter; when melted, add one tablespoonful of flour, stirring constantly; add half a pint of desiccated codfish, which has been soaked for an hour in tepid water. Add a gill of cream and a little pepper, and, if you like, a suspicion of grated nutmeg. Let it all simmer for ten minutes, stirring constantly.—Caterer.

Salpicon of Fish.

CUT cold toast into squares or rounds; lay on each a thick slice of raw tomato; on top of each put some flakes of cold cooked codfish or halibut; cover with a plentiful supply of Hollandaise sauce. Melt a tablespoonful of butter in the chafing-dish; lay in the prepared pieces of toast; cover for about five minutes, and serve.

Hollandaise Sauce.

CREAM quarter of a pound of butter; add yolks of three eggs; beat well together; add the juice of half a lemon and a small saltspoonful of cayenne; stir until smooth and creamy.

Scrambled Codfish.

Put half a pint of cream into the chafing-dish; when hot, stir in half a pint of shredded, well-freshened codfish; let it simmer about ten minutes, then add two well-beaten eggs; stir until they are cooked, add a little white pepper, and serve.

SALT CODFISH HASH.

PUT half a pint of cream into the chafing-dish; add half a pint of mashed potatoes, half a pint of shredded codfish, and a little pepper. Serve when thoroughly heated.

Codfish Tongues.

Put into the chafing-dish a heaping tablespoonful of butter, in which bruise a clove of garlic with a small wooden spoon; take out the garlic; stir in until smooth a tablespoonful of flour, pepper, and salt. Add a pint of Moselle or any white wine and when hot stir in the beaten yolks of two eggs; in this warm the codfish tongues, which have been previously cooked in salted water for about thirty minutes.

Deviled Cod.

MIX a pint of cold-cooked fresh cod, chopped fine, with four hard-boiled eggs, chopped fine. Season with salt, pepper, and a tablespoonful of chopped parsley. Put in the chafing-dish half a pint of cream and a tablespoonful of Anchovy paste; when well mixed and hot, stir in the above mixture and serve.

Salmon Réchauffé.

SEPARATE into flakes a pound of fresh or a can of salmon; pour over it a gill of French dressing made of equal parts of vinegar and oil, a few drops of onion-juice, pepper, and salt. Put in the chafing-dish two heaping tablespoonfuls of butter and a dessert-spoonful of flour; add a gill of cream and a gill of sherry; when well mixed, add the fish and heat thoroughly.

Halibut Sauté.

Have a pound of chicken halibut, cut in thin slices about two inches square, well dredged in flour, pepper, and salt. Put in the chafing-dish three tablespoonfuls of butter. When very hot, put in the fish; as soon as one side is well browned, turn and brown the other. Take out the fish and pour into the chafing-dish the contents of a can of tomato puree; as soon as hot, pour over the fish, and serve.

White Fish à la Provençale.

Put in the chafing-dish two tablespoonfuls of butter; when melted, add one tablespoonful of flour and a gill of milk or cream. Mash fine the yolks of four hard-boiled eggs, which mix well with a teaspoonfuls of anchovy paste; stir constantly until it boils. Add a pound of cold-boiled halibut, cod, or any white fish, cut in small slices, let it simmer a few minutes, and serve.

Sauté of Scollops.

CUT in small pieces half a pint of scollops, which have been previously boiled about fifteen minutes; squeeze the juice of two lemons over them; add half a teaspoonful of cayenne, a teaspoonful of salt, two tablespoonfuls of butter; put all in the chafing-dish. Stir constantly for about ten minutes, and serve.

Scallops en Huile.

Put in the chafing-dish three tablespoonfuls of pure olive oil, salt, a dash of cayenne, six drops of celery extract, and a dessert-spoonful of lemon-juice. Put half a pint of scallops in water at the boiling point (do not let it boil) for five minutes; then drain dry, and dredge with flour by shaking in a napkin. When the oil is *very* hot, add the scallops, and fry quickly.

BOUCHÉS D'HUÎTRES.

ROLL large oysters in pepper and salt; have ready some *very thin* slices of salt fat pork; wrap each oyster in a slice, and fasten with a wooden toothpick. Put in the chafing-dish, and cook just long enough to crisp the pork.

Oysters Sautés.

Select a dozen large, fine oysters, drain the juice thoroughly from them, butter the chafing-dish well, and when *very* hot place the oysters in single layers. When brown on one side turn it upon the other, and brown that also. While cooking, keep adding a little butter; this, combining with the juice given out by the oyster, forms a brown skin in the chafing-dish, and is the very quintescence of oyster flavor. Season with pepper and salt; when nicely browned, serve all, oysters and skin, very hot.—Caterer.

Scolloped Oysters.

PUT in the chafing-dish two tablespoonfuls of butter and a gill of cream; put in a layer of oysters, well drained, and sprinkle over it two tablespoonfuls of cerealine (Cerealine Flakes), another layer of oysters, more cerealine and some small bits of butter; season with pepper and salt. Put on the cover, and cook from five to ten minutes.

Oysters à la Crême.

Put in the chafing-dish two tablespoonfuls of butter, half a pint of cream, a salt-spoonful of salt, same quantity of pepper, a little powdered mace, or grated nutmeg, and two bay leaves. When it boils, sift in two dessert-spoonfuls of *finely* powdered cracker crumbs; add twenty-five oysters, blanched and drained, cook two minutes, and serve on hot toast.

Kornlet Oysters.

Mix with the contents of a can of Kornlet four eggs, well beaten, a little salt and pepper, and a tablespoonful of thick cream. Put in the chafing-dish two tablespoonfuls of butter, and when *very* hot fry the mixture in small portions, about the size of an oyster.

HUITRES EN COQUILLES.

PUT in the chafing-dish three tablespoonfuls of butter and a tablespoonful of flour; when melted and smooth, add half a pint of thick cream, a tablespoonful of grated onion, eight drops of celery extract, and a little parsley chopped fine, a little salt, a dash of cayenne, and the yolks of three eggs. Do not let the sauce boil after the eggs are put in or it will curdle. Pour this sauce into a bowl. Put twenty-five large oysters into the chafing-dish and cook slowly until they are quite solid—thoroughly cooked without shrinking—now pour over then the sauce, and serve quite hot.

Mock Oyster Stew.

TAKE a small piece of salt cod, which has been soaked in cold water over night, and cooked until soft (which should be done by simmering slowly, *not* boiling), shred it fine and mix well with it a tablespoonful of dry flour. Put it in the chafing-dish with two tablespoonfuls of butter, a dozen oyster crackers split; pour over the mixture two cups of hot milk or cream; season with pepper, and stir constantly five or ten minutes.

Sauté of Oyster Crabs.

PUT one tablespoonful of butter in the chafing-dish; when melted, add two tablespoonfuls of thick cream, season with salt and cayenne; when very hot, add half a pint of oyster crabs, cook one minute, and serve.

Crabs Sauté.

PUT into the chafing-dish three tablespoonfuls of butter, a little salt, a salt-spoonful of cayenne, a tablespoonful of lemon-juice, a dessert-spoonful of onion-juice. Now add a pint of crab-meat; (it can be procured in Fulton Market fresh); stir constantly until well heated, and serve at once.

Crabs en Crême.

Put into the chafing-dish half a pint of crab-meat; salt and pepper; serve as soon as hot. It is an improvement to dredge over the meat a little flour while stirring it; let it simmer about five minutes.

Shad-Roe Curried.

Fry in a tablespoonful of pure olive oil a small onion, minced fine; add a teaspoonful of curry, a dash of cayenne, and two tablespoonfuls of thick cream. Cut in slices a shad-roe that has been previously boiled in salted water, and when very hot serve.

HERRING À L'ANGLAISE.

CHOOSE a fat Yarmouth bloater, with a fine soft roe; soak it in milk, skin, and bone carefully, and pound in a mortar with the yolks of two hard-boiled eggs. Put in the chafing-dish a tablespoonful of pure olive oil, a teaspoonful of grated onion, a tablespoonful of tarragon vinegar, and a teaspoonful of paprica; add the above paste and stir until well mixed and hot; serve on toast.

SARDINE TOAST.

PUT in the chafing-dish two tablespoonfuls of butter and one of flour; stir until smooth and a light brown. Add two or three tablespoonfuls of stock, the grated zest of half a lemon, two or three drops of essence of cloves, a wineglass of sherry. Remove the skin from six or eight boned sardines, chop fine, add a teaspoonful of grated onion; stir until the ingredients are thoroughly mixed, and serve hot on toast.

Sardines with Hollandaise Sauce.

Remove the skins from a small box of boneless sardines; add four tablespoonfuls of Hollandaise sauce, and when thoroughly heated serve on toast.

Frogs.

Frogs can be purchased in the market prepared for cooking; cut them in halves, lengthwise; separate the legs. Put three tablespoonfuls of butter in the chafing-dish; when melted, add a tablespoonful of flour, stir until smooth, then add a gill of cream, then the frogs, well seasoned with pepper, salt and a little grated nutmeg. Put on the cover and cook for twenty minutes. A little more cream or milk may be added while cooking.—Caterer.

BEEFSTEAK À LA MODE.

PUT a pound of beefsteak, cut about an inch thick, in the chafing-dish, in which two tablespoonfuls of butter has been melted, with two or three slices of lemon. Let it cook slowly five or ten minutes; then pour over it a gill of good stock, or the same quantity of hot water, in which a dessert-spoonful of fluid beef has been dissolved, also a gill of port wine. Allow the whole to simmer slowly ten minutes longer. When ready to serve, squeeze the juice of a lemon over the steak.—CATERER.

Beefsteak Réchauffé.

CUT in small dice the remains of a good tender steak. Put in the chafing-dish a tablespoonful of butter, two tablespoonfuls of cream, a tablespoonful of Johnston's Fluid Beef; pepper and salt. When hot, add the beef, and serve as soon as hot; do not let it boil. A tablespoonful of mushroom catsup is an improvement.

Hamburg Steak.

ONE pound of beef from the tender part of the round, chopped very fine. Put into the chafing-dish three tablespoonfuls of butter. When melted, a layer of grated breadcrumbs, then a layer of chopped meat; over that sprinkle pepper, salt, a little grated onion, and chopped parsley. Cover closely, and let it cook about ten minutes. Serve hot.

Beef en Matelotte.

Chop very fine six small onions and put in the chafing-dish with two tablespoonfuls of butter; when a light brown, shake in from a small dredging-box about a tablespoonful of flour, stirring all the while. Add a glass of claret, a tablespoonful of stock, a tablespoonful of mushroom catsup, salt, pepper, and two or three drops of extract of celery; lay in the hot-water plate some slices of cold roast-beef, preferably the fillet, and strain over it from the chafing-dish the sauce, prepared as above. Place it over the lamp, closely covered, long enough to heat through.

CHIPPED BEEF.

PUT into the chafing-dish three tablespoonfuls of butter; when melted, stir in a tablespoonful of flour; stir until smooth; add half a pound of chipped beef, which has been soaking for ten minutes in about a gill of water; let it simmer for five minutes, then stir in the beaten yolks of two eggs; serve very hot.

Minced Collops au Naturel.

ORDER from the butcher a pound of beef from the tender part of the round, chopped *very* fine, quite free from fat, skin, etc.; season with pepper and salt; put in the chafing-dish before it is hot; stir constantly until it becomes very hot, to prevent the meat forming in lumps. Sauté it in its own juice for about ten minutes; then add a tablespoonful of butter, a small onion minced *very* fine, a teaspoonful of mushroom ketchup and a tablespoonful of flour made into a smooth paste with a little butter.—CATERER.

Curry of Cold Roast Beef.

Cut some slices of cold roast beef into rather small, square pieces, and dredge them with flour. Chop a small onion fine, and fry it in two tablespoonfuls of butter in the chafing-dish; add a gill of stock, and one tablespoonful of curry powder; put in the pieces of beef, and let all simmer ten or fifteen minutes.

Cold Roast Beef Rechauffé.

Cut cold roast beef in small slices, about half an inch thick; put into the chafing-dish a tablespoonful of butter; when melted, add three tablespoonfuls of currant-jelly, a dash of cayenne, a little salt, and a glass of sherry or Madeira. Add the beef, and serve when hot.

Bubble and Squeak.

Put in the chafing-dish two tablespoonfuls of butter; slightly cook some thin slices of cold corned beef, well peppered; add some cold boiled cabbage, chopped fine, well seasoned with pepper and salt, a tablespoonful of pickled cucumber and onion. mixed, and a small teaspoonful of made mustard; serve hot.

English Stew.

CUT any kind of cold meat, as for hash, sprinkle it with pepper, salt and flour, and lay it in the chafing-dish, in which a tablespoonful of butter has been previously melted, with some pickled cabbage or onions. Pour over it a gill of hot water, in which a tablespoonful of fluid beef has been dissolved, a tablespoonful of mushroom catsup, and a dessert-spoonful of taragon vinegar. Let all simmer for ten minutes, stirring occasionally.

Beef with Jelly.

PUT into the chafing-dish two tablespoonfuls of butter, two of currant jelly, a dash of cayenne, a little grated nutmeg; stir until well blended, then add a gill of sherry. Put in slices of rare roast-beef and let them simmer (not boil) for about five minutes, turning often.

Ragout of Cold Meat.

Put into the chafing-dish a heaping tablespoonful of butter, an even tablespoonful of flour; when melted and smoothly blended, stir in a tablespoonful of grated onion, a tablespoonful of cucumbers (also grated), a tablespoonful of tarragon vinegar, a teaspoonful of finely-chopped parsley, a teaspoonful of paprica, two or three drops of celery extract. Stir until very hot, then lay in slices of either cold veal, lamb, mutton, or chicken.

MUTTON OR LAMB RECHAUFFÉ.

Put in the chafing-dish two tablespoonfuls of butter; when melted, add, stirring constantly, a tablespoonful of flour; add a gill of water; when it boils, stir in a heaping teaspoonful of fluid beef, and one or two teaspoonfuls of mushroom or walnut catsup. Add the cold mutton or lamb cut in small dice, or thin slices, let it simmer about five minutes and serve.

CHOPS WITH MUSHROOMS.

Put in the chafing-dish two tablespoonfuls of butter and one of olive oil, six or eight drops of celery extract, a teaspoonful of onion-juice, pepper and salt; when very hot, put in half a dozen lamb-chops; when brown on one side, turn and brown the other. They will take about five minutes to cook. When ready to serve, pour over them a mushroom sauce that has been very slowly cooking in a little butter and its own juice for half an hour.

Sweet-Breads a là Milanaise.

Mince very fine two sweet-breads that have been carefully prepared and thoroughly parboiled; add a tablespoonful of Parmesan cheese grated, a little salt and cayenne, and the beaten yolks of two eggs; mix thoroughly. Put into the chafing-dish two tablespoonfuls of butter; when very hot pour in the above mixture; let it brown slightly, and serve hot.

Sweet-Bread and Mushroom Ragoût.

Put in the chafing-dish two tablespoonfuls of butter; when melted, two tablespoonfuls of flour, stirring constantly. Season with salt and pepper; add a gill of cream, a cold-dressed sweet-bread, and a dozen mushrooms, cut into small dice. Let all simmer for about ten minutes, stirring often.

Sweet-Breads.

Put two tablespoonfuls of butter in the chafing-dish; when very hot put in the sweet-breads (which have been previously boiled and prepared), cut in small pieces. Cook about five minutes; take out the sweet-breads; add gradually a tablespoonful of flour, pepper and salt, and a gill of cream. Stir constantly until you have a smooth sauce, return the sweet-breads to the chafing-dish, and serve hot.

Veal Cutlets.

Cutlets for the chafing-dish should be previously prepared by dipping pieces cut thin, about two inches square, into eggs, beaten, and seasoned with pepper and salt. After they are egged, dip them lightly into a little grated Parmesan cheese, then into sifted cracker-crumbs. Fry three or four slices of fat salt pork in the chafing-dish. When it is crisp, take out the pork (keep hot) and cook the cutlets in the fat. Serve hot, a piece of pork with each.

Curried Veal.

CUT into small pieces, half an inch square, about a pound of cold roast veal; put in the chafing-dish two tablespoonfuls of butter, an onion, a tart apple, and a clove of garlic, all minced fine; then stir in a tablespoonful of curry powder, and half a tablespoonful of flour; add the meat and pour in half a pint of stock, or the same quantity of hot water, in which a dessert-spoonful of fluid beef has been dissolved. Add a little lemon juice and salt, let it all simmer slowly a few minutes, and serve hot.

Veal Kidneys Sautés.

Put two tablespoonfuls of butter in the chafing-dish; add a small onion, minced fine; when very hot add a veal kidney cut in thin slices; let them cook for about five minutes, turning often. As soon as they are nicely browned, add a tablespoonful of mushroom ketchup, and either a tablespoonful of stock or a dessert-spoonful of fluid beef, dissolved in a little cream. Season with pepper and salt, and, if you like, just before serving, add a glass of Madeira or Sherry.

Ox Tongues, Deviled.

CUT into slices one of Libby, McNeill & Libby's ox tongues; put a layer of them on an ordinary dinner plate, sprinkle over with dry mustard, a little cayenne, and two teaspoonfuls of salad oil; place over this another layer of tongue and season as before. Repeat this until a sufficient quantity of the tongue has been treated; let it remain for three or four hours. Put a tablespoonful of butter in the chafing-dish, and when very hot add slices of tongue, and brown quickly. Add more butter as it is required.

VENISON.

CUT a steak in pieces about two inches square; shake them in a napkin with a handful of flour, to which a little pepper and salt has been added; put three tablespoonfuls of butter in the chafing-dish, and when very hot put in the venison and cook quickly. When done, add half a tumbler of currant jelly; let it melt, and pour over the meat.

Venison Steak.

HAVE the steak cut about an inch and a half thick. Lay it in the chafing-dish, in which two tablespoonfuls of butter have been melted. Season with pepper and salt. Add two gills of port wine, and a tablespoonful of pure red currant jelly. Cook until one side is done, then turn, and cook the other side. The degree of cooking must depend upon your own taste.—CATERER.

Calf's Liver Sauté.

Put in the chafing-dish two tablespoonfuls of butter and a tablespoonful of onion, minced fine. When very hot, add half a pound of calf's liver, cut in slices, well seasoned with pepper and salt and dredged with flour. Sauté on both sides, and serve hot, with a sauce made by beating the yolk of an egg with a tablespoonful of butter, a little cayenne, and a dessert-spoonful of lemon-juice.

FRICANDEAU DE FOIE DE VEAU.

CUT in small dice a portion of calf's liver that has been previously cooked. Put into the chafing-dish two tablespoonfuls of butter and a tablespoonful of flour. Stir until smooth; add a tablespoonful of chopped onion and a teaspoonful of paprica; pepper and salt; add a gill of cream and the liver; let it simmer for about ten minutes. When ready to serve on thin slices of toast, add a tablespoonful of sherry.

LAMB'S LIVER.

CUT the liver in thin slices and the slices into narrow strips; put in a napkin a tablespoonful of flour and a little pepper and salt; put in the liver and shake well until it is thoroughly dredged with flour. Put in the chafing-dish two tablespoonfuls of olive oil, a teaspoonful of onion-juice, and six or eight drops of celery extract. When very hot, add the liver, and cook until a light brown from five to ten minutes.

Pig's-Feet Sauté.

Get from your grocer pig's-feet from the Deerfoot Farm (a set of pig's-feet that are already cooked); have them split in two and rolled in cracker-dust, seasoned with pepper and salt. Put into the chafing-dish two tablespoonfuls of butter, and fry a light brown.

DEVILED HAM.

MIX a large teaspoonful of French mustard, a teaspoonful of tarragon vinegar, a little salt, and a salt-spoonful of paprica. When well mixed, spread over both sides of a slice of cold boiled ham; put a tablespoonful of butter in the chafing-dish, and when very hot put in the ham, and brown quickly on both sides.

Ham à la Fourchette.

IN the hot-water plate melt a tablespoonful of butter; put in a cup and a half of cold boiled ham, minced fine, and half a dozen cold boiled potatoes, sliced thin; put the ham and the potatoes in the plate in alternate layers, and set it aside. Melt two tablespoonfuls of butter in the chafing-dish, stir in a tablespoonful of flour, then add slowly a pint of rich milk; season with pepper and salt; stir in two well-beaten eggs, let it simmer three or four minutes, then pour over the dish of ham and potatoes; remove the chafing-dish, and put the plate over the lamp until it is thoroughly heated—about five minutes.

Ham à l'Espagnole.

PUT rather a thick slice of ham in the chafing-dish, in which you have melted a little butter, brown on both sides, take out the ham and mix with the fat in the chafing-dish two tablespoonfuls of very fine bread crumbs, and half a gill of good cider, not too hard; season with salt and pepper and a little chopped parsley. Mix all well together, put back the ham, and, when hot, serve.

Ham, Piquant Sauce.

MELT in the chafing-dish a tablespoonful of butter, half a teaspoonful of mustard, a salt-spoonful of salt, a salt-spoonful of white pepper, two tablespoonfuls of vinegar and a teaspoonful of tarragon vinegar, half a dozen little pickles and a tablespoonful of capers chopped fine, a teaspoonful of grated onion, and a few drops of celery extract. When hot, stir in the yolks of two eggs. When smooth and creamy, add a pound of finely chopped ham, and serve hot.

Curry Sauce for any Kind of Cold Meat.

PUT two tablespoonfuls of butter in the chafing-dish with one good-sized onion minced fine, eight or ten pepper-corns, a blade of mace, two or three bay leaves. Stir until the onion becomes nicely browned, then add two tablespoonfuls of flour, one tablespoonful of curry powder, a desert-spoonful of vinegar, a pinch of salt, three gills of boiling water, in which a tablespoonful of fluid beef has been dissolved, or the same quantity of good stock. Let all simmer five or ten minutes, stirring constantly. Strain, and stir in any kind of cold meat cut in thin slices, or dice.

Fritadella.

Put in the chafing-dish two tablespoonfuls of butter; cook for about two minutes a tablespoonful of very finely minced onion; add a cupful of bread crumbs, and a cupful of any kind of cold meat minced fine; season with salt, pepper, a little grated nutmeg, and the grated *yellow rind* of a fresh lemon; add half a gill of hot water, in which a dessert-spoonful of fluid beef has been dissolved, or the same quantity of stock. Let all simmer for about five minutes, and just before serving, add two beaten eggs, well stirred in.

TRIPE.

TRIPE should be chosen thick, fat and white, and should be boiled perfectly tender. Put two tablespoonfuls of butter in the chafing-dish; when melted, add a tablespoonful of flour, a gill of cream or a gill of milk; add three or four young onions, chopped fine, pepper, salt and a little made mustard. When well mixed, add half a pound or more of tripe, cut in short strips; let it all simmer about five minutes, and serve hot. A few oysters and a little grated nutmeg are an excellent addition.

Tripe Sauté.

Put two tablespoonfuls of butter in the chafing-dish; when very hot put in half a pound of honey-comb tripe, well boiled, cut in strips about three inches long. When brown on both sides, take out the tripe and add a tablespoonful of flour, a small onion minced fine, and half a pint of cream. Season well with pepper and salt; let it simmer a few minutes, then return the tripe to the chafing-dish, and serve when hot.

Canvas-Back Duck.

TAKE a cold canvas-back, or any wild duck, which has been previously roasted for ten minutes in the oven; divide into suitable pieces; put two tablespoonfuls of butter in the chafing-dish, with two gills of port wine and a little currant jelly; season with pepper and salt, cover the chafing-dish, and cook from five to ten minutes.—CATERER.

Chicken à la Reine.

Put in the chafing-dish a tablespoonful of butter and a pint of the water in which a chicken has been boiled; season with salt and pepper. Mash the yolks of four hard-boiled eggs, and mix with half a cupful of fine bread or cracker crumbs, soaked until soft in half a pint of cream or milk; cut the white meat of the chicken very fine; mix all together, and let it simmer for about five minutes, and serve. If not thick enough, add more bread crumbs.

Chicken Terrapin.

Put in the chafing-dish the dark meat of cold chicken, turkey or grouse, cut in small slice, with half a pint of cream or stock, and when it comes to a boil stir in the following mixture: two tablespoonfuls of butter rubbed into a smooth paste with a tablespoonful of flour and the yolks of three eggs, a teaspoonful of dry mustard, a little cayenne pepper and salt, all mixed with a little cream or stock. Let it simmer a few minutes (not boil), and when ready to serve stir in a large wineglass of Madeira.

SALPICON OF CHICKEN.

ONE cup of cold chicken, minced fine, one cup of boiled macaroni, one cup of tomatoes; add one teaspoonful of paprica and a little salt. Put two tablespoonfuls of butter in the chafing-dish. When hot, add a gill of cream, and then pour in the above mixture. Stir until well heated, and serve immediately.

Canned Chicken.

Richardson & Robbins' luncheon bread. Take carefully from the can in solid shape; cut in slices, dip them in beaten egg, then in sifted cracker-crumbs. Put three tablespoonfuls of butter in the chafing-dish, and when very hot lay in the slices of chicken; cook until brown.

Salpicon Imperial.

Put in the chafing-dish two tablespoonfuls of butter; when melted, stir in a heaping tablespoonful of flour; pour over gradually half a pint of broth and half a pint of cream. Add a small onion, a small bunch of parsley, a bay-leaf, and a blade of mace, all chopped fine; let it simmer from ten to fifteen minutes, stirring often. Put in the hot-water plate the breast of a chicken (previously cooked), cut in small dice, and a sweet-bread, also cooked; cut in dice; pour over it all through the strainer the sauce, made as above. Put the plate over the lamp until well heated, and serve immediately with croutons of toast.

Poulet aux Champignons.

Put into the chafing-dish two tablespoonfuls of butter and a tablespoonful of flour. Stir until smooth; add six mushrooms, sliced, and cook slowly ten minutes; now add half a pint of cream, pepper and salt, a teaspoonful of grated onion, and a very little grated nutmeg. Add a pint of cold chicken, chopped fine, and simmer about fifteen minutes longer, stirring often.

Pic-ca-dee.

ONE pint of chopped meat, any kind of white meat, fowls or game; one can of tomatoes after the juice has been drained off, one onion, chopped fine or grated; one half pint of cream, a teaspoonful of salt, a pinch of cayenne, a few drops of celery extract. Put into the chafing-dish a large tablespoonful of butter. When hot, add the above mixture; cook ten minutes, stirring occasionally; then add two well-beaten eggs; cook five minutes more, and serve with hot toast.

Salmi of Game.

Put the remains of a roast partridge in the chafing-dish, with a small piece of raw ham chopped fine, and a small onion chopped fine. Put in a little lace bag, containing a clove of garlic (bruised), three bay leaves, three cloves and a blade of mace. Add half a pint of water, and let it all boil slowly half an hour. Remove the sac aux fines herbes, add two tablespoonfuls of butter, made into a smooth paste, with one tablespoonful of flour and a glass of white wine. Stir constantly a few minutes and serve.

SALPICON OF TURKEY.

ONE pint of turkey meat, minced fine; a large sweet-bread, minced fine; a teaspoonful of grated onion, a teaspoonful of lemon; salt and pepper to taste; heat in the chafing-dish a large cup of cream and two tablespoonfuls of butter; when this is boiling stir in a tablespoonful of flour mixed with a little of the cream reserved for that purpose; add the meat, and when that has cooked about two minutes stir in two beaten eggs; cook four or five minutes longer, and serve hot with toast.

Capilotade of Turkey.

Cut up the remains of cold roast turkey in small pieces. Put in the chafing-dish two tablespoonfuls of butter; when melted, add two tablespoonfuls of flour, stirring constantly until smooth; season with pepper, salt, and a tablespoonful of chopped parsley. Add half a pint of stock or cream, put in the pieces of turkey, with five or six mushrooms; let it all simmer for about ten minutes; just before serving, add a glass of wine.

SALPICON OF GAME.

TAKE remains of duck, grouse, or quail and cut in small pieces. Put two tablespoonfuls of butter and a tablespoonful of flour in the chafing-dish; stir until brown; add a teaspoonful of tomato catsup and a tablespoonful of mushroom catsup, a teaspoonful of grated onion, salt, pepper, and two or three drops of celery extract; now add the meat, and serve when hot with croutons of toast.

SQUABS.

HAVE squabs prepared as for broiling. Put three tablespoonfuls of butter in the chafing-dish, pepper and salt, and a few drops of celery extract. When very hot, pour into the dish three squabs and cook until a light brown on one side, and then turn and cook the other side. Serve immediately.

Reed Birds.

Put in the chafing-dish three tablespoonfuls of pure olive oil, six drops of celery extract, a little salt and pepper. When very hot, add the reed birds and cook from five to ten minutes.

Reed Birds in Blankets.

WRAP the birds in very thin slices of salt larding pork; fasten with wooden tooth-picks; fry them in the chafing-dish until the pork is crisp, turning constantly.

JAMBON À BON GOÛT.

ONE cup of finely-chopped cooked ham, one of grated bread-crumbs, two cups of hot mashed potatoes, one large table-spoonful of butter, three eggs, a pinch of cayenne; mix all well together; put a dessert-spoonful of butter into the chafing-dish. When hot, pour in the above mixture, cover, and let it remain about ten minutes. Serve with Hollandaise sauce.

PETIT POIS.

PUT two tablespoonfuls of butter in the chafing-dish; when melted, add a can of French peas; season with pepper and salt. Let them cook for about ten minutes.—CATERER.

Potato Soufflée.

MIX a pint of mashed pototoes with half a cup of thick cream and the whites of two eggs, beaten stiff. Put two tablespoonfuls of butter in the chafing-dish, and when very hot put in the potatoes in large tablespoonfuls. When brown on one side, turn, brown the other, and serve immediately.

Potatoes à la Lyonnaise.

Put two tablespoonfuls of butter into the chafing-dish; when melted, add two or three onions, chopped fine; cook two or three minutes; then add half a dozen cold-boiled potatoes, sliced, well seasoned with pepper and salt; sauté a nice light brown. Just before serving, add a tablespoonful of finely chopped parsley.

Potatoes Rechauffé.

Cut half a dozen cold-boiled potatoes into slice; put in the chafing-dish with a tablespoonful of butter and half a pint of cream; let it simmer about five minutes and then stir in a teaspoonful of lemon juice, a little chopped parsley, pepper and salt, and the beaten yolk of two eggs; let it simmer (not boil) and serve hot.

Lima Beans.

Add to a pint of young Lima beans, previously boiled and seasoned with butter, salt and pepper, half a pint of freshly gathered mushrooms. Put a tablespoonful of butter in the chafing-dish; when melted, add beans and mushrooms with half a gill of cream; let it all simmer for about ten minutes, and serve hot.—Caterer.

Fried Tomatoes.

CUT fine, ripe, solid tomatoes in halves; dredge them with pepper, salt, and sifted cracker dust. Put three tablespoonfuls of butter in the chafing-dish; when very hot, cook the tomatoes on both sides and serve. A little onion juice is an improvement.

Tomatoes and Mushrooms.

Add to a pint of tomatoes, previously cooked, half a pint of mushrooms, a heaping tablespoonful of bread crumbs, a tablespoonful of butter; season with pepper and salt, and simmer for a few minutes, long enough to cook the mushrooms, and serve on slices of buttered toast.—Caterer.

SAUTÉ OF MUSHROOMS.

PUT in the chafing-dish two tablespoonfuls of butter; when melted, add a tablespoonful of flour, stirring constantly. When smooth, add salt, pepper and a tablespoonful of lemon juice, a little mushroom ketchup, and half a pint of boiling water, in which a tablespoonful of fluid beef has been dissolved. Add the mushrooms, and boil until tender.

MEADOW MUSHROOM.

IN selecting this mushroom crisp and heavy ones should be chosen in preference to light and soft ones, as being less likely to become leathery in cooking. Cut the mushroom across and remove the stem; put in the chafing-dish two tablespoonfuls of butter; put in the mushrooms, and cook them at the lowest possible temperature from fifteen to twenty minutes, or even longer; a great heat destroys the flavor.

Puff Ball.

ONE of the most valuable of the edible mushrooms. Remove the outer skin, cut in slices half an inch thick, season them with pepper and salt, dip the slices in the yolk of an egg and then in finely-sifted cracker-dust; put three tablespoonfuls of butter in the chafing-dish, and when very hot fry slowly, and serve immediately.

AGARICUS CAMPESTRIS.

PUT in the chafing-dish two tablespoonfuls of butter and half a pound of the mushrooms, cut in thin slices; cook slowly for fifteen minutes, then add a gill of thick cream, pepper, and salt, and cook slowly ten minutes longer. Serve immediately. Prepare the mushrooms by peeling; the stem can be scraped, cut in thin slices, and cooked with the rest.

Fairy Ring Champignon.

Put in the chafing-dish two tablespoonfuls of butter and one of flour; when smooth, add half a pint of thick cream; when hot, add a pint of the mushrooms and stew slowly from fifteen to twenty minutes; add pepper and salt, and serve hot on toast.

CANTHARELLUS CIBARIUS.

SELECT this mushroom with care, avoiding a deleterious species called cantharellus aurantiacus. Put in the chafing-dish three tablespoonfuls of butter, a pint of mushrooms, pepper, and salt. Cut the mushrooms across, remove the stems, and cook very slowly.

MUSHROOMS WITH BACON.

FRY five or six slices of bacon in the chafing-dish. When nearly done add a dozen good-sized mushrooms and fry them slowly until they are cooked. In this process they will absorb all the fat of the bacon, and, with the addition of a little salt and pepper, will be found most appetizing.

Mushrooms à la Provençale.

Steep for two hours in some salt and pepper a pint of mushrooms. Put in the chafing-dish a tablespoonful of butter, a teaspoonful of lemon-juice, a little finely-chopped parsley, and a teaspoonful of grated onion. When the mushrooms are ready cook them slowly five or ten minutes.

MACARONI AU GRATIN.

PUT into the chafing-dish two tablespoonfuls of butter and half a pint of grated cheese; now add a pint of well-boiled, well-drained macaroni, and stir all together until the cheese is melted, when serve at once.

Tomato Purée and Macaroni.

Fry a clove of garlic or a few slices of onion in two tablespoonfuls of butter; when brown, remove the garlic and stir in a tablespoonful of flour; stir in a small can of tomato purée, and when thoroughly heated add a cupful of macaroni, which has been previously cooked, and half a pint of finely-minced cold veal. Stir constantly until it is thoroughly heated and well mixed. Season with salt and pepper.

Dried Beef with Eggs.

Put two tablespoonfuls of butter in the chafing-dish, with two gills of cream or milk, and a quarter of a pound of dried beef, shaved very thin; let it simmer for about ten minutes, then stir in rapidly three or four eggs; serve as soon as the eggs are set.

Eggs à la Jardinière.

Put into the chafing-dish two tablespoonfuls of fresh butter; when melted, add a tablespoonful of chopped mushrooms or truffles. Season with pepper and salt; add four or six eggs, beaten slightly. Stir constantly, until set, about two minutes, and serve hot, on toast.

OMELET.

BEAT three fresh eggs slightly with two tablespoonfuls of cream; season with pepper and salt. Put a tablespoonful of butter in the chafing-dish, and when very hot, pour in the egg, holding the dish by the handle in the left hand; scrape up rapidly from all parts of the pan the cooked egg, letting the liquid portion follow the knife. The moment it is sufficiently cooked, which will be in forty to fifty seconds, slip the knife under the left edge and fold the omelet over rapidly, gently, and neatly to the side of the pan opposite the handle. Have ready a warm oval plate, reverse it on the pan, turn pan and plate over quickly together, and the omelet will rest on the plate.

Tomato Omelet.

MAKE the omelet according to directions on the preceding page. Just before pouring it into the pan, add very solid pieces of tomato, cut in small dice, over which a little onion has been grated. Season with a little cayenne.

CURRIED EGGS.

PUT two tablespoonfuls of butter in the chafing-dish; mince two small onions very fine, and cook until they begin to brown; stir in two dessert-spoonfuls of curry powder, mix well, and add two tablespoonfuls of flour, stirring quickly all the time; then add half a pint of veal or chicken stock, or the same quantity of boiling water, in which a tablespoonful of fluid beef has been dissolved. When the mixture has simmered gently for about ten minutes, add two tablespoonfuls of cream and six hard-boiled eggs, cut in slices. When well heated through, serve.

FRICASSEED EGGS.

PUT two tablespoonfuls of butter in the chafing-dish; when melted, add a tablespoonful of flour, stirring constantly, a sprig of parsley, cut fine, five or six minced mushrooms, half a pint of white stock, veal or chicken, or the same quantity of cream, in which a dessert-spoonful of fluid beef has been dissolved. Simmer about five minutes, and add six hard-boiled eggs, cut in thick slices; boil up once, and serve hot.

Eggs á l'Espagnole.

PUT in the chafing-dish a tablespoonful of the best olive oil, in which cook a clove of garlic, chopped very fine; add three sliced tomatoes, half a dozen sliced mushrooms, two or three slices of smoked beef tongue, minced fine. When *very* hot, add three or four eggs, beaten slightly, stirring rapidly all the time. As soon as the eggs are set it is ready to serve.

CREAMED EGGS.

Cut hard-boiled eggs in quarters, lengthwise; make a rich, white sauce in the usual way—two tablespoonfuls of butter and one of flour; when smooth, add half a pint of cream and half a pint of milk or white stock, a little finely-chopped parsley, and a dash of nutmeg; put in the eggs, and, when thoroughly heated, serve.

Eggs à la Maître d'Hôtel.

PUT in the chafing-dish two tablespoonfuls of butter; when hot, stir in three or four onions, cut very fine, and cook until a light brown. Add a tablespoonful of flour, stirring constantly, a small cupful of cream or milk, a little finely chopped parsley, pepper and salt. Add six hard-boiled eggs, cut in quarters. When hot, serve.

Scrambled Eggs.

Put a tablespoonful of butter in the chafing-dish, pepper and salt; when hot, add a gill of cream and six eggs. Stir constantly for two or three minutes. Serve immediately on hot toast.

Scrambled Eggs en Huile.

Put into the chafing-dish two tablespoonfuls of pure olive oil; add eight drops of celery extract, a dash of cayenne, a little salt, a tablespoonful of parsley, chopped fine, and a teaspoonful of onion-juice. Stir until well blended and hot, and then add six eggs, which have been already broken but not beaten. Stir constantly until they are well cooked, and serve at once.

Ham and Eggs.

Put two tablespoonfuls of butter in the chafing-dish; when melted, add half a pound of lean, boiled ham, cut in small dice, a little pepper, a tablespoonful of chopped chives or onions, add six, eight or ten eggs. Stir constantly until the eggs are cooked.—Caterer.

Welsh Rarebit.

Put a tablespoonful of butter in the chafing-dish; when nearly melted, add a pound and a half of fresh cheese, cut in small dice, a teaspoonful of dry mustard, a little cayenne; *stir all the time;* add a small amount of ale or cream to prevent burning. Keep adding ale or cream, about half a pint in all. Serve hot on toast.

Cheese Fondu.

Put a tablespoonful of butter in the chafing-dish; when melted, add a cup of fresh milk and a cup of fine bread crumbs, two cups of grated cheese, a salt-spoonful of dry mustard, a little cayenne. Stir constantly, and add, just before serving, two eggs, beaten light.

Cheese Crouton.

PUT in the chafing-dish two tablespoonfuls of thick cream, a tablespoonful of butter, half a pint of grated cheese, a salt-spoonful of paprica, and half a salt-spoonful of salt. Work these ingredients to a smooth paste and spread on toasted bread or crackers.

Cheese Soufflé.

Put in the chafing-dish two tablespoonfuls of butter and half a pint of grated cheese (any good cheese will do); add two tablespoonfuls of thick cream, salt, and a pinch of cayenne. When melted, stir in three well-beaten eggs. Stir continually until the eggs are cooked, and serve immediately.

Paprica Welsh Rarebit.

Put in the chafing-dish a tablespoonful of butter; when melted, add a pound of grated cheese (American cream); as the cheese melts, stir in gradually about a gill and a half of ale, or, if preferred, rich milk; add a dessert-spoonful of paprica. Mix well, and serve very hot on toast.

MACARONI À LA GRUYÈRE.

PUT into the chafing-dish with two tablespoonfuls of butter half a pint of grated cheese (half Gruyère and half Parmesan), a salt-spoonful of white pepper, a gill of cream, and a very little nutmeg; salt to taste; now add a pint of cold, well-boiled macaroni. Stir well, let simmer for five minutes, and serve hot.

Beignets de Pommes.

Take some soft, tart apples, peel and remove the pips; cut in round, thin slices; plunge them in a mixture of brandy, lemon juice and sugar, until they have acquired the taste; drain them, dust them with flour. Put in the chafing-dish three table-spoonfuls of butter; when *very* hot, fry the slices on both sides, sprinkle powdered sugar and cinnamon, and serve very hot.

Bread Sauté.

CUT the crust from a thick slice of bread; put in the chafing-dish two tablespoonfuls of butter; when very hot, brown the bread on both sides, take it out, and put in two tablespoonfuls of grated ham, two tablespoonfuls of grated cheese, and a gill of cream; season with cayenne pepper. Mix all well together, and when very hot spread the mixture on the toast.

Warren's Prune Toast.

CUT the crust from rather a thick slice of Vienna bread; put in the chafing-dish two tablespoonfuls of butter, and, when very hot, brown the bread on both sides. Pour over this half a pound of Warren's Prunes, which have been previously boiled long enough to enable you to remove the pits. Sweeten to taste. Add a glass of sherry, and serve with cream.

CREAMED ANCHOVY TOAST.

SPREAD six slices of toast from which the crust has been cut first with butter and then with anchovy paste; put in the chafing-dish half a pint of cream; put in the toast, and baste constantly with the cream until very hot.

CAVIARE.

PUT in the chafing-dish four tablespoonfuls of cream; when hot, add the contents of a can or box of caviare; when thoroughly heated, serve very hot on nicely-browned slices of toast with quarters of lemon.

Wheatena for Breakfast.

Pour, very slowly, one measure of Health Food Company's Wheatena into six measures of slightly salted, *actively* boiling water. Boil one minute; serve with cream and sugar. If to be served cold, use seven measures of water instead of six, and pour the mush into moistened moulds. Turn out when cold. It can also be cut in slices and fried in butter in the chafing-dish. I cannot praise too highly this delicious cereal.